The Handbook to Unleash Your Potential Using Six Practical Steps

Contents

Praise for Toyinda & The Handbook to
Unleash Your Potential Using Six Practical Steps

"My mom helps me unleash my potential; she pushes me and encourages me to do what I need to do to be successful."

Tristan L. Wilson, Son and Future Engineer

"No matter how many successes you've attained, there will always be an opportunity for new achievements as long as you're living with intention. Revisiting proven principles helps you to release your latent ability continually. In 'Unleash Your Potential,' Toyinda unpacks practical steps that you can use along the way."

"I am excited for Toyinda; here is where the student becomes the teacher."

Adrian Warren, Your A-Game Success Coach
#warrenwisdom, mrawarren.com

"When I was a college athlete at 19, I was given these words of wisdom, "Visualize yourself on that podium as a champion. Then, make it so." It was the first time I was ever told to see myself as a champion and leader...to visualize it so clearly in my head, then strive to make it a reality. These words didn't come from a coach; they came from my very own teammate, Toyinda Smith. Even at 19, she inspired others to become their very best, and she continues to this day. Her words have stayed with me some 20 years later as I raise my daughters and teach them how to unleash their potential. And they will undoubtedly stay with you, too." #togetherwestand

Amy Moyer, Vice President, Action for Healthy Kids, 1999 T&F All-American, 1996-97 Purdue Co-Captain

"I first met Toyinda when her collegiate track & field team travelled to the University of Washington to compete against our team. Of course, I didn't let her unleash potential on me. Years later, Toyinda held a special luncheon to raise money for throwers who needed shoes, and I was the keynote speaker. Toyinda is a woman who saw a great need to encourage the throwers in track and field and saw that the most significant need was for proper throwing shoes – she was positioning them to reach their potential. She set about raising money, for the throwing shoes, in her community. She met her goal of supporting all her throwers with a new pair of shoes. When I was in high school I did not have money for throwing shoes; my high school coach helped keep me in the shoes needed for my throwing events. I admire Toyinda for her perseverance. Perhaps after reading Toyinda's book, more people will not be afraid to address the needs they see and feel empowered to search out ways to serve the needs of their community in the same way that she does."

Aretha Thurmond, Four-time Olympian & Managing Director of International and Championship Teams, USATF

"If you are ready to be unleashed and get moving in your purpose, this book is just for you! God divinely ordered meeting Toyinda. After speaking with her about my

4

passion and purpose, there was an instant connection, and she began to encourage, push, and assist me with my dreams. As one of my mentors, I have seen her inhale and live out loud the words penned in this book. My life continues to evolve because of her bold faith moves. If you want to see change, allow this book to be the tool that awakens your potential, so you can live in your purpose, and transform the world."

Char-Michelle McDowell, Founder & CEO of The B.R.A.G. Collection™ and The Well Consulting Firm™

"As the Head Women's Track Coach at Purdue University, I had the great fortune to work with many outstanding student-athletes. In college you can recruit talent to your team and the better they are coming in, generally, the more success they have. However, one of my greatest success stories was Toyinda Smith who was a walk-on to my team. Toyinda was a decent discus thrower in high school, and I knew it would take some time for her to develop. Practicing the six steps she mentions in this book, she would go on to be one of the greatest athletes in Purdue history and a national champion. Toyinda proved that through good coaching and just as importantly determination, courage and a never quit attitude, one can accomplish great things. And that is what she can bring to your organization. The knowledge that only someone who has been there can truly know and understand."

Benjamin Paolillo, former Head Women's Track & Field Coach, Purdue University

"The fourth step in *The Handbook to Unleash Your Potential* is to enlist. It's been said that "one's eyes show the strength of the soul." Not only does Toyinda's eyes show strength, her voice, and presence command a room, her actions show leadership, and she exudes confidence. Along her way to unleash potential, she has been able to directly and indirectly enlist individuals onto her team. Toyinda has been my mentor, friend, big sister, and teammate since 1993. I've followed in her footsteps since our high school days. Toyinda has been right by my side along the way. When we strive to become better than we are, everything around us becomes better too—because of Toyinda I am better. My potential is unleashed!"

Darria Clayton, Track & Field Teammate, Soror, Friend

"It is with delight and sense of privilege to endorse Toyinda Smith in her drive and calling to help others reach their full potential. Early on Toyinda was recognized as an outstanding student-athlete in track and field and demonstrated the drive and desire to excel at all levels in NCAA competition. That same drive and passion are still evident today. While teaching Leadership Development at Purdue University, I was privileged to have Toyinda as one of my most determined and enthusiastic students. After graduation, we stayed in contact, and I watched her grow and develop in her leadership experience, and she demonstrated her drive and leadership in new professional assignments. In her new book, she shares her continued ambition and excitement in helping others reach their potential. As a recognized leader in sport and now a business professional with an endorsement as a John Maxwell Certified Leadership Trainer, Toyinda demonstrates new leadership renewal and potential in her training sessions, her performance, and in her shared vision to help others grow. She has a great story to tell and ***The Handbook to Unleash Your Potential Using Six Practical Steps*** will provide new insights and tools in reaching your full leadership potential."

Rodney Vandeveer, Professor Emeritus,
Purdue University

"Toyinda lives leadership personally and professionally. Toy knows that we all have greatness and success within us and that we are often fearful of this inner strength. She will help you discover the power you hold to become your best self. She will then provide you tools to challenge yourself to achieve your potential for yourself and for the communities you choose to serve."

Richard Puffer, Executive Director, Byerly Foundation & Professor Emeritus of Communication, Coker College

"I had the opportunity to work with Toyinda as her throws coach at Purdue University. The first characteristic she displayed to me was very goal-oriented with the desire to work hard towards obtaining those goals. She showed talent in the discus throw and learned the weight throw as her career progressed. When competing, I observed the quiet and determined way she approached winning the competition, following precise steps. During her career at Purdue, she unleashed her potential and became B1G Conference and NCAA Division-I Weight Throw

Champion. Read the handbook, do the work, unleash your potential!"

Gene Edmonds, former Volunteer Assistant Women's Track & Field Coach, Purdue University

"CEO, Toy Smith, has provided expert consultative service to our school and parent organization. She has a keen eye in determining relevant, meaningful, and effective solutions for our organization. As an entrepreneurial endeavor, our school is constantly changing and evolving. As such, we need quick and accurate solutions that can help maintain the integrity of our vision, unleash our potential and achieve our goals. CEO Smith has helped us do just that! Her consulting firm has moved various projects including internal and external communication and parent training and workshops. As a result, we have more synergy within our organization. We are proud to work with Leadership Strategy & Consulting and look forward to what the future holds."

E. Keith Bailey, Executive Director, Pee Dee Math, Science, & Technology Academy, Pastor & Author

Foreword

Unleash Your Potential, is undoubtedly a manual to have because it has so many great and practical principles, that will help bring to fruition, what's on the inside of you. Many of us have heard about ourselves, and we've said concerning others, that there's so much potential. However, many of us never see the fulfillment and cultivation of these manifold aspects of our lives because we don't have the next steps or the how-to, in order to make the connection between where we are and where we want to be; based on what we know and see inside of us. Toyinda Smith, a great strategist, and leader provides six steps that will help you unleash this potential; which will help many to reach self-actualization according to Abraham Maslow's, *Hierarchy of Needs Theory*.

It is certainly a great blessing that you have even allowed me to partake in this process of you releasing your potential as a writer and author. I'm forever grateful that you've entrusted me to be a part of this great project.

De'Angela Haynes, Ph.D. and Author of Encourage Yourself in the Lord (2010)

Acknowledgements

I don't take it for granted that I have truly been blessed with gifts, talents and the will to achieve the goals that I have established in my personal, spiritual and professional life. I thank God for allowing me to leave my voice in the earth realm using this handbook as a vehicle. I appreciate the God I serve for increasing my faith in him and faith in my abilities to succeed, even after countless failures.

Thank you to everyone that has sown and poured into me including my amazing inner circle of business and sports coaches, natural and supernatural mentors, intercessors, sorority sisters, teammates, trusted advisors, colleagues, friends and family members. Your encouragement mattered, especially when you pushed me to #stayinthepress™ on the days that I felt defeated and dejected.

To Mary and Homer Smith, Jr., I'm so blessed to have excellent parents like you, although I have not verbalized it, I continue to learn from your provision, togetherness, and individuality including the different balance you bring between the three. Thank you Aryal and Tristan, my two very insightful little people, you inspire me to rise to my best possible self each day. I am proud of you and your accomplishments!

Introduction

"One isn't necessarily born with courage, but one is born with potential."

- **Maya Angelou**

You are born with potential! You are born with potential! You are born with potential! Now that that's clear, it is essential to make clear in your mind that for you to achieve in any domain that you must do something. My sorority sister and high school teammate, TK Farmer, recently presented a speech at a sports conference and she shared a concept that is unassuming, yet weighty. The following is what she exclaimed. "You've got to do something to do something!" Wow! What if you would actually do something? Execute! Activate! Implement! Do it! When our mindset shifts from comfortable to uncomfortable we reach capacity – our "do something" zone. The zone that allows our potential to be unleashed.

As the Principal at Leadership Strategy & Consulting, LLC, a team and leader development firm aimed at equipping women, teams, and organizations to be champions, I have spent the past 4 years positioning people to win in productivity, team engagement, communication, transformational leadership, obtaining remarkable results and execution. I have found that the most successful people achieve, not because they are talented, educated, or financially stable (although you need this). They achieve because they are persistent with their attempts to win at life.

My purpose in writing this book is to move you from stagnation to action, encourage you to make good better, make the better your best, build wealth through triumphs, and create a pipeline for legacy building. Additionally, I want to introduce you to success strategy that if diligently followed will position you to truly unleash potential. Unleashed potential doesn't just stop at personal; you can unleash your potential in business, ministry, sports, civic engagement and academics as well. If you do the work, you will accomplish your goals, objectives, dreams, and visions quicker and with more confidence than ever before.

As you move through this handbook your passion will be re-fired, your mindset will be re-wired, and you will be re-set, placed back on a championship track. The method, should you decide to follow it, requires you to think, write, prioritize, enlist, activate and reflect. Business minded people can advance by intentionally implementing the six steps. Ministry leaders will find that they are not working from a place of spontaneity but a place of calculation. Sports teams will learn that winning becomes easier through being deliberate in actions. Organizations will influence their followers because they will take the time to establish plans.

If you expect this to be easy, you will stop when you are subjected to any unfavorable experience. If you expect this to be overly challenging, more than likely, you won't even exert the effort it takes to cause your potential to manifest into positive results. In this handbook, I will bring to your attention fears that are causing you to be stationary. I will challenge your current process of achieving. I will pronounce traps that you may fall into that will cause you not to have forward movement. I will provide exercises for you to work so that you can get a jump start on success.

You are born with potential; it will take courage and poise for you to unleash it!

Chapter 1
WHAT IS POTENTIAL?

It's gratifying for me to experience living out my personal mission. That personal mission is merely to make a positive impact, doing something that makes a positive impact. Developing this handbook is just one avenue that I am using to accomplish my personal mission. It's a way for me to unleash my potential and to bring others along the way.

Potential is a point in your life, profession, business and even ministry, where something innovative is on the cusp of being made manifest. It's not entirely displayed, almost hidden to the world. Potential can be described as something pioneering, likely to happen. Potential is a flower in the garden that is budding, but it's not quite to fruition; however, it's peering out – an impending fully realized flower. For the flower to unleash potential, the owner of the flower must be willing to invest time in thinking about the growth plan for the flower. The flower must be breathed upon, it must be visualized, watered and sunlight must shine upon the vision.

That growth plan must be written down in a journal, for example, a vision board, or even a note card that's placed in a prominent and frequented location. In most cases, since the owner of the flower has many other obligations, it makes perfect sense for a prioritization model to be put in place. Even after the owner of the flower has arranged their priorities, no one does anything great alone. We are talking about potential being unleashed. The owner must ask for the right type of help because just any warm body won't do. In other words, the owner must be very strategic in choosing his/her team. Create a team of vision pushers. Vision pushers are those who share the vision, to bring the flower to fulfillment. When the team is in place, you've got the start the work and keep inspired to action. Through the movement of the owner first and then the team, the flower's potential is unleashed and now must be revisited, for possible suggestions about whether to improve the process or continue as is. Once the flower is realized, it can be used in advanced ways such as for pollination, weddings, gifts, and even landscaping décor.

Do you have an "it," a dream, vision, objective or focus that you "need" to release? I use the term "need" because it's essential that you actualize "it" to advance and expand your purpose, passion, and position. Expansion is really about growth, and if you are not growing, you're dying. I repeat, when you stop growing, you are dying. Your life comes to a stalemate – you remain stagnant and suppressed. Let me say it this way. Decomposition sets in the minute you stop growing. The science that studies decomposition is generally referred to as taphonomy. Taphonomy comes from the Greek word taphos, which literally means TOMB. The minute your personal, professional and spiritual self stops growing, it begins to decompose and breakdown which means that you are headed for a personal, professional and spiritual **tomb**.

Back to my question. Do you have an "it," a dream, vision, objective or focus that you need to unleash? I know that the answer is yes, otherwise you will not have invested in this resource.

Now that I am convinced you have an "it," if you can do it, the thing that you have dreamed of doing – name that "it."

Write "it" below. You may have several. Be very specific.

_____

_____

_____

_____

_____

_____

_____

_____

_____

_____

_____

_____

_____

_____

_____

_____

_____

Chapter 2
FEAR NOT

What is stopping you from accomplishing it? Is it fear, distractions, a lack of resources, not enough education, an inadequacy of time in the day?

I read a very enlightening passage in John C. Maxwell's book, *The 15 Invaluable Laws of Growth,* that talked about why people do not succeed. The reading suggests that people have several fears that become barriers to their potential being unleashed. [1]

The first fear is of failure. I understand that this can be a real concern as I experienced a type of failure regarding both my marriages ending in divorce. Those experiences caused me to feel not only disappointment, frustration, sadness, and regret, but also a deep shame. I've learned that shame makes people feel bad about who they are versus feeling bad about the action. Shame is terrible because our self-esteem and identities begin to come under attack. In order to move beyond shame, I restructured my thoughts, consistently used positive self-talk and prayed until I became free of the negative feeling of shame. Freedom feels good!

The second fear is of going from security to the unknown. I know this all too well. I worked in higher education for over 14 years and knew when I would receive my paycheck. I took a risk and left the institution to pursue my own consulting firm. There were many times when I did not know when I would receive a paycheck, or even an opportunity to earn a paycheck. Now that's unknown!

The third fear suggested is the fear of what others may think about you, your goals or aspirations. As people, we worry about disappointing people whose opinions we value. I have been consulting for four years now; it took me four years to be confident in not needing the approval of others, in fact, I feared the release of new projects because I believed that people would not take my firm or me seriously. What a waste of valuable time.

The last fear I will mention is a fear of losing friends. My thought here is that we can only control aspects of our own lives. Be okay with friends shifting as mobility begins to occur in your personal and professional life. By the way, the "good book" tells us to "fear not" at least 365 times. That's one time a day for the year. We must go from information to transformation! "Fear Not!" So, what's stopping you from unleashing your potential?

Write "it" here. What has you at a stalemate? What will you do about it? Be specific.

_____

_____

_____

_____

_____

_____

_____

_____

_____

_____

_____

_____
_____
_____
_____
_____
_____
_____
_____
_____

Okay, one more question before we get into the six practical steps to position you to unleash your potential. Answer this question. Are you willing to sacrifice to accomplish "it?" A sacrifice is a surrendering of something, for the purpose of something else. When you are on the journey to unleash potential, you may be required to give up, for example, time, treasure, and talent. It's a part of the process to be successful.

Are you willing to sacrifice? List what sacrifices you are willing to make. Be specific.

_____
_____
_____
_____
_____
_____
_____
_____
_____
_____
_____
_____
_____

Chapter 3
BEFORE POTENTIAL...
THREE PRACTICES

Now that you have committed to the process let's get started. I know you want to do, be and have more. Part of the commitment is your ability to discipline yourself, your thoughts and your actions. A requirement is that you focus and activate self-empowerment. This means that you will take action in being intentional about the process of controlling your own life. I'm talking about an external process which builds your self-esteem and confidence in your ability to make good decisions to govern your life to achieve self-sufficiency and options that expand you.

To empower yourself, I suggest you implement three practices with unwavering persistence. The first practice that you must implement with unwavering persistence is positive and accurate thinking. Positive like the little blue engine. In Watty Piper's 1930 children's book, *The Little Engine That Could*, the engine convinced herself by declaring, "I think I can, I think I can."[2] And she did.

Your thoughts are mighty, they have the ability to create and terminate. Consider the law of attraction. Byrne (2006) suggest that "the law of attraction is forming your entire life experience, and this all-powerful law is doing that through your thoughts. You are the one who calls the law of attraction into action, and you do it through your thoughts."[3] Indeed a notion to contemplate.

The accompanying practice with positive thinking is accurate thinking. Accurate thinking is like the 1960's commercial where a boy finally asked an owl, how many licks does it take to get to the tootsie roll center of a tootsie pop. The owl grabbed the tootsie pop, tested it himself and developed an accurate answer of three licks. As you know, I'm being humorous. Accuracy here means that you weigh what could go wrong and you are accounting for that through your deliberations. You must make sure your thoughts do not have thinking errors embedded.

The second practice that you must implement with unwavering persistence is desire. You must have the desire to be, have and do more. You must know what you want and crave accomplishment until it is complete. During my undergraduate years in college, I had the opportunity to complete two independent studies, in the Psychology Department that specifically focused on the "motivation," within rats. Those experiences influenced my success because they taught me to apply the concept of "drive," – the innate urge to attain a goal or satisfy a need, to my everyday life. I discovered that the rats' behavior changed drastically when they had a craving versus when they were satiated. When the rats were hungry, they stopped at nothing to fill the void, regardless of the setbacks. From that experience, I learned that I had to have a passion. I had to be hungry if I planned to unleash my potential in life.

As an entrepreneur, I have learned that desire turns into a decision; decision determines direction which translates into the reality and whether the potential is unleashed or bottled up due to satisfaction with where you currently are. The former CEO of Xerox, Ursula Burns, is an example of someone with the desire to be self-empowered to unleash potential. She is the first black woman to head a Fortune

500 company. Burns was raised by her mother in the rough public housing projects on the Lower East Side of Manhattan. In an article, she said, "Many people told me I had three strikes against me: I was black. I was a girl. And I was poor. However, my mother reminded me where you are, is not who you are."[4] What an inspiring example of unleashed potential.

The third practice that you must implement with unwavering persistence is the right type of activity. As you are aware, all activity will not equal you unleashing your potential. If we go back to the flower example, had the owner of the flower walked past the flower without watering it for weeks, the flower would have withered away. Your potential will not be actualized if you do not focus your behaviors on the efforts that will get you the highest return on your investment. The return is unleashed potential!

You cannot do everything, and you must concentrate on your desire to reach potential. Some people disagree with me when I say, "you cannot do everything." However, Michael LeBoeuf, business consultant, author, and retired management professor, once said, "devoting a little of yourself to everything means committing a great deal of yourself to nothing." I believe this is true as I have had to make tough decisions not to activate every talent that I occupy. It's uncomfortable, but I must sacrifice so that my own potential is unleashed. You must be a disciplined person with disciplined actions.

How will you discipline yourself, thoughts and actions? What will manifest due to you being disciplined? Be Specific.

_____

_____

_____

_____

_____

_____

_____

_____

_____

_____

_____

_____

_____

_____

_____

_____

_____

_____

_____

_____

_____

Chapter 4
THE FIRST PRACTICAL STEP: *THINK*

The First Step to Unleash Your Potential: *Think*

As business owners, leaders and creatives we must sit down in quiet spaces and think. Don't just think about anything; use your mind to think about accomplishing your purpose and passion. What are you thinking?

What are you thinking as it relates to accomplishing your purpose and passion? Be Specific.

_____
_____
_____
_____
_____
_____
_____
_____
_____
_____
_____
_____
_____
_____
_____
_____
_____
_____
_____
_____
_____

I asked what you were thinking because your thoughts can shape and shift your world. According to Claude M. Bristol, author of *The Magic of Believing*, he believes "thought is the original source of all wealth, all success, all material gain, all great discoveries, and all great achievements."[5] You must be deliberate about what you are thinking. Deliberation starts with creating a safe place to think about your goals without the interference of distractions. This is a prerequisite for birthing amazing aspirations leading to unleashed potential.

Distractions can be concrete, such as your social media notifications, children needing attention, lack of basic needs, etc. However, there is one abstract distraction that you must pay close attention to, and that is limiting beliefs. I encourage you to remove the "limiting belief" chatter that we allow to enter into our cognition because of past experiences, especially the negative occurrences.

One way to do this is to consider self-efficacy. Self-efficacy is emphasized by Psychologist Albert Bandura (1994) in the journal article entitled, *Self-Efficacy*. He defines self-efficacy as "one's belief in one's ability to succeed in specific situations or accomplish a task."[6] Given that, self-efficacy plays a crucial role in how you think and then behave. What you believe and verbalize about your capacity to attain, undoubtedly is a deciding factor in whether you fail or succeed. If this is an area of your life that needs to expand, Bandura suggests that we should master our experiences by performing tasks successfully. Also, he states we should invest time with others who are doing what we want to do, this is called social modeling. Finally, he asserts that social persuasion, meaning receiving verbal encouragement from others will help you to break through the barrier of self-doubt. I have experienced a limiting belief distraction, luckily self-efficacy prevailed. After I graduated from college, I decided that I would compete in track and field post-collegiately. That aspiration was short lived as I discovered that I was pregnant and could only continue training up until a particular stage in the pregnancy. I took twenty-two months off from track and field training, for the weight throw.

During my "break" from track and field I moved into the third trimester of my pregnancy and after that, birthed my daughter. However, soon after my daughter was born and upon the release of my doctor, I decided that I wanted to give track and field one more try. Limiting belief chatter began to flood my thoughts. Aren't you too old? Shouldn't you be at home nurturing your child? What will others say? Haven't you been resting too long? I curtailed the chatter and decided that to "come back," I had to believe firmly in my abilities to succeed and commit to doing the work. I sat in a quiet place to think. Then, I wrote out my vision. Next, I prioritized my objectives. After that, I enlisted a coach and started the training. Finally, I reflected on the entire process.

I worked and thought my way back up to my collegiate distance in the weight throw. I went to the 2002 United States of America Track & Field (USATF) Indoor Nationals (the meet where elite athletes including USA Olympians compete) in New York to contend in the weight throw. I had a great series of throws and placed 3rd with a distance of over 70 feet. I celebrate this because I broke my collegiate best by more than 2 feet. I believed in my ability to succeed and did not let the distraction of limiting beliefs cause me to be inactive.

What concrete and limiting belief distractions do you have? What will you do to gain victory? Be Specific.

_____

_____

_____

_____

_____

_____

_____

_____

_____

_____

_____

_____

_____

_____

What do you believe about your abilities? Be Specific.

_____

_____

_____

_____

_____

_____

_____

_____

_____

_____

_____

_____

_____

_____

_____

_____

_____

_____

_____

_____

Snares to Thinking

1. You begin thinking about the wrong things.
2. You are confused about your purpose.
3. You are wondering rather than thinking.

Chapter 5
THE SECOND PRACTICAL STEP:
WRITE

The Second Step to Unleash Your Potential: *Write*

There is a great passage that states one must write out the vision, so that those who read it may carry out the vision. Write down everything. You must start by purchasing a journal that you will use for the one purpose of unleashing your potential, after that, start writing. You must write your ideas and thoughts on paper mainly because your memory is suspect. Some people with children can't even remember their names. Your ideas don't remain in your head for long. Your written words bring clarity and focus to what you should be doing. All of your thoughts matter and they matter most when they are written on paper. As ideas, concepts, and considerations come to you write, don't scratch ideas from the list. Focus on one subject at a time.

Consider brainstorming, a technique that I require teams of people to use when developing solutions to problems, stimulating creative thinking and amassing information. Brainstorming can be solitarily executed and is best when you are on the journey to unleashing potential. Alex Osborn popularized the term brainstorming in his book, *Applied Imagination.* Osborn advocates that for the brainstorming session to be useful you must not immediately judge what you write on the list, expand and increase the list and try not to brainstorm with multiple questions.[7] Choose one question in the session. Your question should be, "What do I desire to accomplish in this year?"

What do you want to accomplish this year? Be Specific.

_____

_____

_____

_____

_____

_____

_____

_____

_____

_____

_____

_____

_____

_____

_____

_____

_____

_____

_____

Snares to Writing

1. Your concentration is off.
2. You don't know where to start.
3. You have lack of ambition.

Chapter 6
THE THIRD PRACTICAL STEP:
PRIORITIZE

The Third Step to Unleash Your Potential: *Prioritize*

Now that you have developed your list of thoughts, visions, and objectives, prioritize the list. After you have created your list, categorize it. Categorizing is a part of critical thinking, your ability to think clearly about what approach to take next. Prioritizing allows you to arrange and then commit to the tasks that are imperative to your success in this season. What should you do first, second, third and so on? Many prioritization models can be considered when trying to unleash potential. I suggest the Pareto Principle, named after Italian Economist and Sociologist Vilfredo Pareto. This is a principle studied in business and known widely as the 80/20 rule. The principle states, "For many events, roughly 80% of the effects come from 20% of the causes."[8] Put another way, when you focus on the top 20% of all your priorities you will get an 80% return on your effort. In order to reach your goals, you will have to focus and turn this prioritization principle into practice. Examples that I can think of to make this concept clearer may look like this.

✓20% of the donors give 80% of the donations
✓20% of the athletes score 80% of the points
✓20% of the ideas create 80% of the results

When you begin to prioritize you have to commit to follow-through no matter what tries to vie for your attention. Evaluate your priorities. I have been consulting for four years. I have made investments in my consulting business by enrolling in growth and development programs. The insight that I have used focuses on "what I must do." For example, I have spent a great deal of time building a "know, like and trust factor" with potential clients in the Pee Dee region of South Carolina. As the founder, it was my responsibility to be visible - the face of the company. That was a must do.

As you begin considering your responsibilities, think of it in this way. What do I have to do and what can I possibly assign to others? I understand that priorities shift. However, I learned to consider investing time in activities and services within my business that gives me a high financial return both from a short and long-term perspective.

Compartmentalize your priorities with the 1-3-5 Productivity Rule. Using this rule allows you to focus on both the big picture and small details of your priorities enabling you to execute an easy to manage method. But, don't forget to assess how long it will take you to complete your priorities.

Here is what the 1-3-5 Productivity Rule suggests.

1.) Commit yourself to accomplishing 1 massive goal.
2.) Decide on 3 activities that will help you achieve the 1 massive goal.
3.) Identify 5 strategies that will help you to accomplish the 3 activities.

Another use of the 1-3-5 Productivity Rule is below.

1.) Create 1 thing you must do.
2.) Identify 3 things you need to do.
3.) List 5 things you want to do.

Also, the 1-3-5 Productivity Rule can be used as such.

1.) Complete 1 large task.
2.) Complete 3 medium tasks.
3.) Complete 5 small tasks.

I have shared with you three approaches to tackling your priorities to increase productivity. Most people who want to unleash potential will consider using the strategies in seven areas of life including family, career, spiritual, personal, financial, physical health and mental health.

Prioritize your top thoughts, goals or objectives from your list. Next to each one, write out what your return on investment will be. Then, write out how long it will take you to accomplish it. Be specific.

_____

_____

_____

_____

_____

_____

_____

_____

_____

_____

_____

_____

_____

_____

_____

_____

_____

_____

_____

_____

_____

_____

_____

_____

_____

_____

Snares to Prioritizing

1. You are not disciplined.
2. You are not passionate about what's on the list.
3. You decide that other responsibilities are more important.

Chapter 7
THE FOURTH PRACTICAL STEP: *ENLIST*

The Fourth Step to Unleash Your Potential: *Enlist*

Who can you recruit to assist you in actualizing your priorities? It is important to consider the people with which you are already connected. These are people that you can relate to, possibly people in your profession. These are people who can help you accomplish your goals. Do not be nervous; activate your confidence and reach out to them. I have often heard that "the fortune is in the follow through." This statement is true for me as out of following up with individuals after networking events, I gained business contracts, and opportunities I would have not otherwise received.

As an illustration, when I moved to South Carolina from Indiana, I attended an event out of town (15 minutes away) that I was hesitant to participate in, mainly because I knew that I would be one of few people that looked like me there. I mustered up enough confidence to not only go but to converse with the people at the event.

As I was eating my shrimp cocktail, two gentlemen joined me where I stood. I introduced myself and shared with them my business card. I also shared my athletic background, the desire to coach track and field and explained that I had not long ago moved to South Carolina. One of the men was president of a local school that had an opening for head track and field coach. At the end of our conversation, I asked for their business cards and followed up via email shortly after the event. The school president responded to my message by letting me know that he had spoken to the athletic director about my desire and if I wanted to be interviewed that I should submit my credentials. I followed through, interviewed and was hired.

This is just one of many personal examples from my experiences. "The fortune is in the follow through!" In general, most people want to help us succeed. It's critical that you don't select random people. Select trusted people that you have developed relationships with overtime. Trusted people want to see you excel. They are people that you can potentially help, have helped or have served with at some point in your life. It is also important to not limit your reach. A trusted advisor may not be in your field. However, they may know of someone in your domain and can make an introduction for you. This is a perfect example of acting on your behalf.

I want to share a concept that I learned from author, vice-chairman and managing director at Morgan Stanley, Carla Harris, by watching her in a video. Harris stated that people who want to achieve need an advisor, a mentor, and a sponsor. These people make up your personal board of directors. To maximize your potential, you need an advisor, a person you ask distinct questions to and share the significant achievements that you are obtaining.

Additionally, in order to maximize your potential, you must have a mentor. This is a person you can trust to tell the great things, the not so great things and things that are indifferent. Your mentor should be positioned to give you personalized advice and when you meet with your mentor, don't waste their time, come ready with questions. The final person on your personal board of directors should be a sponsor. This person is someone who is going to champion your cause. What does that look like? Your sponsor is the person that is going to go into a professional meeting to speak on your behalf. The sponsor is a person of influence. You may even have to create a list of people with which you must reconnect. Create a personal board of directors.

Bob Beaudine, in his book, *The Power of Who*, gives a few reasons why we should not go to just "anybody" to get the help we need. First, he states, "Anybody doesn't really care about your dream." Second, "Anybody isn't reliable, they usually give advice that is convenient." Third, "Anybody doesn't know you personally, so they are too busy with their own agenda to stop and help you."[9] If you want to unleash your potential, you must be willing to let your guard down and reach out to trusted people. Ask for help!

You have prioritized your top thoughts, goals or objectives. Below, list out the top three and next to each one list three trusted advisors that you believe can assist you in reaching each of those goals. Be specific.

_____

_____

_____

_____

_____

_____

_____

_____
_____
_____
_____
_____
_____
_____
_____
_____
_____
_____
_____
_____

Write out the name and contact information for the people you will enlist. Next to each, list a timeframe for when you will make contact. Be specific.

_____
_____
_____
_____
_____
_____
_____
_____
_____
_____

Snares to Enlisting

1.   You are afraid to be rejected.
2.   You don't want to be vulnerable.
3.   You ask the wrong people.

Chapter 8
THE FIFTH PRACTICAL STEP:
ACTIVATE

The Fifth Step to Unleash Your Potential: *Activate*

It is now time to start the work. There is a huge gap between knowing what you should be doing and doing what you should be doing. You must bridge the gap. When you consider the start of new work, you must also consider that you are not perfect and there will be challenges and frustrations in the journey. It is a part of the process of unleashing your potential. It is essential that you do not operate in a flawless mindset. That's unrealistic.

To start, I suggest you become aware of your strengths, limitations, motivations and what drives you to begin and end a project. You can begin to understand your strengths and limitations by completing a personality typing assessment such as Real Colors® or StrengthsFinder. After completion, seek the help of a skilled professional to assist you with making sense of the outcomes. Those assessments will give you a better understanding of how you achieve remarkable results. Below are descriptions of the two assessments that I'm trained to use when working with individuals, teams and organizations.

Real Colors® Personality Typing Indicator can help individuals, teams and organizations discover how the four temperaments, typical to all people, influence them as individuals and their work atmosphere, collaborations, and team chemistry. The StrengthsFinder Assessment, on the other hand, is a tool that uses intentional questions to facilitate the understanding of your most prominent strengths, and which ways to best get the most out of them both personally and professionally. By knowing these strengths, reaching objectives becomes transparent with strategic techniques for enhancing and bettering your talents. At the center of it all, you must understand your purpose and have an unwavering passionate drive to fulfill it.

Napoleon Hill in his book, *Think and Grow Rich*, put it well, I think, when he said, "Behind this demand for new and better things there is one quality one must possess to win, and that is *definiteness of purpose* – the knowledge of what one wants and a burning desire to possess it."[10] If you really want to unleash your potential, you must have a desire to do the work. You can't unleash potential and remain dormant at the same time. It won't work.

What are your strengths and limitations? What training, knowledge or skills must you add to be positioned to unleash potential? List any programs, books or professional development activities that will equip you to fill in your gaps. Be Specific.

_____
_____
_____
_____
_____
_____
_____
_____
_____
_____

_____

_____

_____

_____

_____

_____

_____

_____

_____

_____

What fears might you have with starting? What lies are you telling yourself? What is the truth? Use a black ink pen. List the fears and lies that you have been rehearsing. Now, use a red ink pen. Next to each fear and lie, write out the truth. Be Specific. Each day, read aloud what you have written in red. Discipline yourself to come into agreement with the truth.

_____

_____

_____

_____

_____

_____

_____

_____

_____

_____

_____

_____

_____

_____

_____

_____

_____

_____

_____

Snares to Activating

1. You have a few of the four fears mentioned.
2. You will not persist.
3. You don't dare to take the risk.

Chapter 9
THE SIXTH PRACTICAL STEP:
REFLECT

The Sixth Step to Unleash Your Potential: *Reflect*

After we have executed the steps to unleash potential the final step is assessing whether to pivot or pursue. The best way to make an informed decision is to set aside time to reflect. While you are on the road to unleash your potential, the ability to reassess, revisit and reevaluate your personal and professional experiences are vital to your ability to advance and expand. There are a few questions that are important to consider when moving through the reflection process.

1. How did you invest your focus in being successful?
2. What outcomes did you want and what did you get?
3. What methods did you use to complete the work?
4. How did your trusted advisors assist?
5. What would it look like if you had to do it over?

Critiques come to help us to advance and improve. For instance, supervisors provide performance evaluations to bring to your attention where improvements in work are necessary for success. They are also in place to acknowledge your accomplishments. Be bold enough to reflect and give yourself a performance evaluation. Below are a few more questions I ask myself during my reflection process.

1. How did I perform?
2. How did I reach the results I wanted?

3. How can I improve?
4. What am I doing that can be assigned to someone?
5. What did I do that didn't give me the expected return on investment?
6. Did I estimate the right amount of time for my top priorities? How do I know?
7. Did I ask the right people for help? How do I know?
8. How did I best utilize my personal board of directors?

There are so many growth benefits connected to practicing reflection, including making informed data-driven decisions. Di Stefano et al., 2014, in their article, *Learning by Thinking: How Reflection Improves Performance*, reasoned that learning from direct experience can be more effective if coupled with reflection. The researchers determined three things: (1.) the intentional effort to express and understand lessons learned from practices allows for an increase in learning for future progression; (2.) reflecting on what has been learned makes experiences more productive and (3.) reflection builds one's confidence to achieve a goal.[11] To unleash your potential, you will need to make a commitment to reflect as a means of advancement and performance improvement.

During this process (working through the six steps), how did you invest your focus towards being successful? Give yourself a performance evaluation. Be specific.

_____
_____
_____
_____

_____

_____

_____

_____

_____

_____

_____

_____

_____

_____

_____

_____

_____

_____

Snares to Reflecting

1.   You are not disciplined enough to do the work.
2.   You don't want to face the harsh facts.
3.   You will not calendar the time to reflect.

Chapter 10
UNLEASHED POTENTIAL

"Once you understand your why, the pressure in the pursuit becomes worth it! That's true in business, athletics and in your personal life."

– Toyinda L. Smith

I have unleashed my potential in many capacities. I resigned from a 14-year career in higher education to be an entrepreneur. I have moved my family over 700 miles away from immediate family, friends and established connections. I have created a presence with my balloon décor company in a new region. I unleashed my potential by rebranding myself in a new state. I'm currently growing my consulting firm and offering expanded services. Finally, I am a published author. The results didn't happen instantly, and it won't for you either.

Beyond the list above, my fondest example of unleashing potential comes from my track and field days at Purdue University. Back in college, I was invited to unleash my potential as a discus thrower with the women's track and field program. I remember the phone call I received in 1994 while in my residence hall room. That's when we were still using landlines. I answered my phone, and the head track and field coach shared that he had seen me throw in high school and wanted to invite me to walk onto the team. I was excited and fearful – this was the B1G Conference. I pulled confidence up and excitely said yes, I would join the team.

The initial step in joining the team was the completion of paperwork with the National Collegiate Athletic Association's (NCAA) Clearinghouse. After that process, I was informed that I qualified partially – a Proposition 48 Athlete. This meant that I had to pay attention to my academics, sit out from competition, lose an athletic competition year, train alone and not officially wear the university team uniform. During this timeframe, in hindsight, I realize that I practiced the six practical steps. I sat in my room and thought about what I wanted to accomplish. After that, I purchased a spiral bound notebook (my rendition of a journal) and started to write out my vision of actually being a contributing member of the team. As well as adding to our team winning the leagues' team championship and carrying a decent grade point average.

Later, I prioritized what I needed to do first, second and third. Subsequently, I enlisted people on campus who could help me be my best and hold me accountable to meet my priorities. Activation came next, studying, conditioning, throws training and a lot of checking in with my academic and athletic advisors. Finally, my year of sitting out was completed, I reflected on how I invested my focus towards being successful. With the help of my throws' coach, Gene Edmonds, below are the compounded results of my potential being unleashed over my time as a student-athlete. Thank You Coach E!

Five-time B1G Champion; Two-time Runner-Up; Third Place Finisher; Two-time All American; NCAA Division-I Champion and; Two-time Hall of Fame Inductee.

Your potential can be unleashed in athletics, business, ministry and civic domains; but you have to do the work. **Are you willing to do the work?**

As you move beyond stagnation to action, positioning yourself to achieve more in life, take note of small wins. As we discussed in chapter four, every small victory builds our confidence.

List your small wins and the date of completion. Be specific. Let's celebrate!

_____

_____

_____

_____

_____

_____

_____

_____

_____

_____

_____

_____

I want to hear your success stories. Join 'The Handbook to Unleash Your Potential' Facebook Group, where we can encourage each other through the process of unleashing potential. Also, sign-up to receive my newsletter and complimentary leadership education located on my membership site at www.toyconsults.com.

Notes

1. John C. Maxwell. *15 Invaluable Laws of Growth* (New York: Hachette Book Group, 2012), 12.

2. Watty Piper. *The Little Engine That Could* (New York: The Platt & Munk Co. Inc., 1930), 17.

3. Rhonda Byrne. *The Secret Law* (New York: Beyond Words, 2006)

4. Julia Horowitz, "Former Xerox CEO Ursula Burns: Government Needs to Help Uplift the Poor," http://money.cnn.com/2017/07/18/news/ursula-burns-american-opportunity, August 5, 2017.

5. Claude Bristol. The Magic of Believing, Success Manual Strategist Edition. (New Jersey: Princeton Cambridge Publishing Group, 2010), 45.

6. Bandura, Albert, (1994). Self-efficacy. In V. S. Ramachaudran (Ed.), Encyclopedia of human behavior (Vol. 4, pp. 71-81).

7. Osborn, Alex F. Applied Imagination: Principles and Procedures of Creative Thinking. New York: Scribner, 1953

8. Kevin Kruse, "The 80/20 Rule and How it Can Change Your-Life," https://www.forbes.com/sites/kevinkruse/2016/03/07/80-20-rule/, May 8, 2017.

9. Bob Beaudine. The Power of Who. (New York: Center Street, 2009), 25.

10.Napoleon Hill. Think and Grow Rich. (New York: Penguin Group Inc., 2005), 24

10. Giada Di Stefano, Francesca Gino, Gary Pisano & Bradley Staats, "Learning by Thinking: How Reflection Improves-Performance,"

https://hbswk.hbs.edu/item/learning-by-thinking-how-reflection-improves-performance, December 20, 2015.

About the Author...

Toyinda L. Smith is purposeful, passionate and persistent. As well as an entrepreneur, leader, and champion influence™ infuser. After 14 years of serving in leadership capacities at Purdue University, she founded Leadership Strategy & Consulting, LLC where she specializes in guiding individuals and groups – particularly women, teams, and organizations – to be champions in leadership, athletics, education and business.

Toyinda is an energizing speaker who stirs teams to increase productivity in every way. She weaves personal and professional anecdotes into her talks inspiring attendees to action. She provides trainings to organizations, higher education institutions and businesses on such topics as employee engagement, becoming a coaching leader, temperament identification, emotional intelligence, support staff empowerment and advancing team goals. As a coach, she equips, educates and empowers people to start or enhance their coaching practice through the champion influence™ coaching certification program.

Toyinda's leadership extends into her community as she serves as CEO and President at Legacy of Women, a non-profit organization in place to inspire the hearts of women towards meaningful giving, healthy living, and transformational leading. She is an active member of Sigma Gamma Rho Sorority, Incorporated where she strives to impact the quality of life for women.

She is certified to facilitate the Real Colors® Personality Instrument, trained to integrate Clifton StrengthsFinder Assessment, is a certified Leadership Speaker, Trainer, and Coach with the John Maxwell Team, serves as a track and field coach and teaches public speaking at a local college in South Carolina.

Toyinda earned an associate degree in organizational leadership and supervision and double bachelor's degrees in psychology and sociology at Purdue University. She has a master's degree in student affairs and higher education from Indiana State University. She has two amazing children ages fifteen and fourteen.

Be sure to visit her website. Sign up to receive complimentary leadership education and join the membership site: www.toyconsults.com.

ADDITIONAL THOUGHTS...

ADDITIONAL THOUGHTS...

Made in the USA
Columbia, SC
10 May 2021